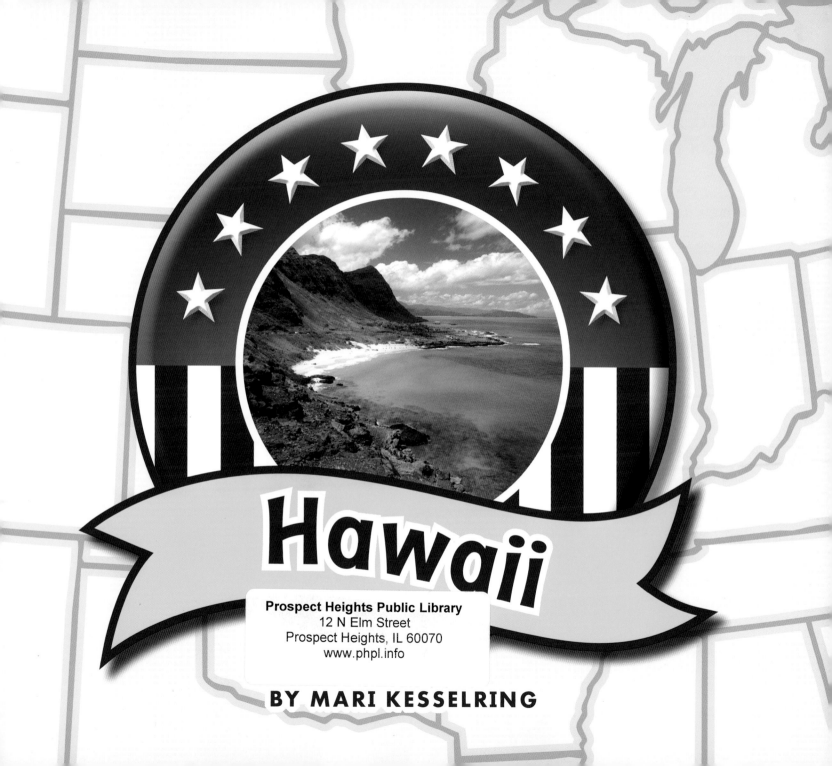

Hawaii

BY MARI KESSELRING

The Child's World

Published by The Child's World®
1980 Lookout Drive • Mankato, MN 56003-1705
800-599-READ • www.childsworld.com

ACKNOWLEDGMENTS
The Child's World®: Mary Berendes, Publishing Director
The Design Lab: Design and production
Red Line Editorial: Editorial direction

PHOTO CREDITS: Henry Price/iStockphoto, cover, 1, 3; Matt Kania/Map
Hero, Inc., 4, 5; Philip Dyer/iStockphoto, 7; S. Greg Panosian/iStockphoto,
9; iStockphoto, 10, 11; Jose Gil/Shutterstock Images, 13, North Wind Picture
Archives/Photolibrary, 15; Bobby Schutz/iStockphoto, 17; Hans Pennink/
AP Images, 19; Drazen Vukelic/Shutterstock Images, 21; One Mile Up, 22;
Quarter-dollar coin image from the United States Mint, 22

LIBRARY OF CONGRESS CATALOGING-IN-PUBLICATION DATA
Kesselring, Mari.
  Hawaii / by Mari Kesselring.
    p. cm.
  Includes bibliographical references and index.
  ISBN 978-1-60253-455-1 (library bound : alk. paper)
  1. Hawaii—Juvenile literature. I. Title.

  DU623.25.K47 2010
  996.9—dc22

                              2010017674

Printed in the United States of America in Mankato, Minnesota.
July 2010
F11538

On the cover:
The landscape
of Hawaii
is a mix of
mountains and
beaches.

CONTENTS

Geography

Let's explore Hawaii! Hawaii is located more than 2,000 miles (3,219 km) southwest of California. It is a group of many islands. The state is surrounded by the Pacific Ocean.

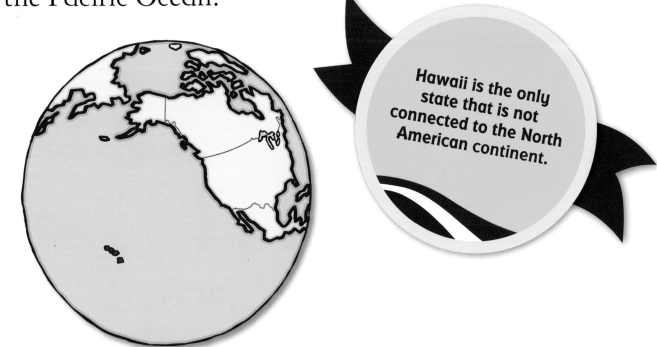

Hawaii is the only state that is not connected to the North American continent.

Pacific

Ocean

Niihau

Kauai

Kaumakani

Wahiawa

Oahu

Pearl Harbor

Honolulu

Diamond Head

Kualapuu

Molokai

Lanai

Lanai City

Lahaina

Maui

Hana

Kahoolawe

HAWAII

Kailua-Kona

Hilo

Hawaii

Pacific

Ocean

Cities

Honolulu is the capital of Hawaii. It is also the largest city. Honolulu is on the island of Oahu. Hilo is the second-largest city. It is on the island of Hawaii.

The eight largest islands of Hawaii are Hawaii, Kauai, Kahoolawe, Lanai, Maui, Molokai, Niihau, and Oahu.

Honolulu is located by the ocean. ▶

Land

Hawaii is a group of eight large and 124 small islands. **Volcanoes** formed these islands. **Lava** from the volcanoes cooled and became hard. It built up from the ocean floor until it was above the water. Hawaii has mountains and valleys. The state has many sandy beaches.

In Hawaii, beaches and mountains are often right next to each other. ▶

Plants and Animals

Hawaii has many plants and trees. Flowers here open up all year long because of the warm weather. The state flower is the yellow hibiscus. Many birds that live in the state are found nowhere else in the world. The state bird is the nene (NAY-nay). It is also called the Hawaiian goose.

The yellow hibiscus grows 3 to 15 feet (.9 – 4.6 m) tall. ▶

The nene is an endangered species. This means there are not many of these birds left in the world.

People and Work

More than 1 million people live in Hawaii. Most people live in Honolulu. Hawaii is a **popular** place to visit. Many people work in **tourism**. Hawaii is an important place for the U.S. **military**. Many people who live here work in the military. Other people work in farming or fishing.

Some people in Hawaii entertain tourists with Hawaiian dancing. ▶

History

The first people to live in Hawaii came from other islands in the Pacific Ocean around the year 300. An explorer from Europe came to the islands in the late 1700s. The United States claimed Hawaii in 1898. On December 7, 1941, Japan attacked Pearl Harbor, Hawaii. After this, the United States joined **World War II**. Hawaii became the fiftieth state on August 21, 1959.

Fishing and water transportation were ▶
important to coastal villages.

Several kings ruled Hawaii before it became part of the United States.

15

Ways of Life

People in Hawaii value the **culture** of their state. Some people still speak the native Hawaiian language. People also enjoy this state's warm weather. **Surfing** is one popular activity. Hawaii is known for the hula and leis. The hula is a type of dance. A lei is a necklace that is usually made of flowers.

A surfer rides a wave on the Pacific Ocean. ▶

Famous People

U.S. President Barack Obama was born in Honolulu, Hawaii. He became the first African-American president of the United States in 2009. Actor Nicole Kidman was also born in Hawaii. She was in the movies *Moulin Rouge!* and *The Golden Compass*.

President Barack Obama waves to a crowd as he exits his airplane. ▶

Famous Places

Visitors to Hawaii enjoy its many beaches. Looking at the state's volcanoes is also popular. The USS *Arizona* **Memorial** is in this state. It honors the people who died during the Pearl Harbor attack.

Diamond Head volcano in Honolulu erupted about 300,000 years ago. ▶

State Symbols

Seal

King Kamehameha I is shown on the Hawaii state seal. He was one of Hawaii's kings. Go to childsworld.com/links for a link to Hawaii's state Web site, where you can get a firsthand look at the state seal.

Flag

The eight horizontal stripes on the Hawaii state flag stand for the state's eight largest islands.

Quarter

The state quarter also displays King Kamehameha I. The quarter came out in 2008.

Glossary

continent (KON-tuh-nunt): A continent is one of the seven large land masses on Earth: Asia, Africa, Antarctica, Australia, Europe, North America, and South America. Hawaii is not connected to the North American continent.

culture (KUL-chur): Culture refers to the art and manners of a group of people. Hawaiian culture is very important to many Hawaiians.

endangered species (en-DAYN-jurd SPEE-sheez): An endangered species is an animal or plant that is in danger of dying out. The nene, the Hawaiian state bird, is an endangered species.

lava (LAH-vuh): Lava is the hot, liquid rock that comes out of a volcano. Cooled lava built up to form Hawaii.

memorial (muh-MOR-ee-ul): A memorial is a place or thing that honors people or events. The USS *Arizona* Memorial is in Hawaii.

military (MIL-uh-tayr-ee): The military is the armed forces of a country. Some people in the military live and work in Hawaii.

popular (POP-yuh-lur): To be popular is to be enjoyed by many people. Hawaii is a popular state to visit.

seal (SEEL): A seal is a symbol a state uses for government business. A former king of Hawaii is on the state's seal.

surfing (SURF-ing): Surfing is riding big waves on a long board. Surfing is a common sport in Hawaii.

symbols (SIM-bulz): Symbols are pictures or things that stand for something else. The seal and flag are symbols of Hawaii.

tourism (TOOR-ih-zum): Tourism is visiting another place (such as a state or country) for fun or the jobs that help these visitors. Many people in Hawaii work in tourism.

volcanoes (vol-KAY-noz): Volcanoes are places in the ground, often on top of mountains, from which lava, steam, and ashes shoot. Hawaii was made from volcanoes.

World War II (WURLD WOR TOO): World War II is the war fought from 1939 to 1945 between the Allies, including the United States, and the Axis powers, including Germany and Japan. The United States entered World War II after Japan attacked Pearl Harbor.

Further Information

Books

Goldsberry, U'ilani. *A is for Aloha: A Hawai'i Alphabet*. Chelsea, MI: Sleeping Bear Press, 2005.

Taylor-Butler, Christine. *Hawaii*. New York: Children's Press, 2007.

Web Sites

Visit our Web site for links about Hawaii: *childsworld.com/links*

Note to Parents, Teachers, and Librarians: We routinely verify our Web links to make sure they are safe and active sites. So encourage your readers to check them out!

Index